FAITH IN

RICHARD EYRE

Darton, Longman and Todd
London

This edition first published in 1992 by
Darton, Longman and Todd Ltd
89 Lillie Road, London SW6 1UD

First published in 1990 by
Churchman Publishing Limited
117 Broomfield Avenue
Worthing, West Sussex BN14 7SF

ISBN 0-232-51983-8

A catalogue record for this book
is available from the British Library

Printed and bound in Great Britain
at the University Press, Cambridge

Contents

Preface

This book attempts to explore as honestly as possible what faith in God is in itself. There are many books which set out *what* we believe, but not so many which invite us to consider the nature of faith itself, how it can be justified, what it is, what strengthens it, and what attacks it. There are also many misconceptions current about it, which can prevent people recognising the faith which in truth they have, and part of the purpose of the book is to dispel these.

What I have tried to write about faith in God stands at certain points in clear debt to the majestic and magisterial work of Hans Küng, *Does God Exist?* I am also specially grateful for the writings of John Macquarrie, whilst I have long owed a great deal to Dom Georges Lefebvre's *Simplicity, The Heart of Prayer* which has nourished both mind and prayer.

RICHARD EYRE

For all seekers, that they may find and be found.

CHAPTER 1

The Phenomenon of Faith

Of those who read this book or even just idly handle it, it is probable that nineteen out of every twenty will count themselves as having faith. That is to say, it is more likely to be read by those who already share something of the faith of which it speaks than by those who do not share it or who explicitly deny it. If that is indeed so, it may be thought regrettable or disappointing. If a case is to be made for faith in God, should it not best be read by those who are dubious that any such case can be made? But we cannot draw a clear line between believers and unbelievers. A wise professor of philosophy once reminded an audience entirely composed of believers: 'There is an unbeliever concealed within each one of us.' It is harder, and possibly more odious, to claim that there is a man or woman of faith concealed within each unbeliever. Nor would such a claim accord with the honesty at which this book aims. Honesty, we have all been told, is the best policy – a counsel of enlightened expediency. But when it comes to a discussion of the meaning of faith and the possibility of faith in the world of today, honesty is not simply the best, but the only, policy. It is needed by those who have faith in order that they may commend that faith to those who have not found their way to it. Whilst the commendation must be supremely in their lives, they must not be found wanting when called to account for that faith. So perhaps it is no great loss, if what is written here is read more by the faithful than by the faithless. Nevertheless, it has chiefly in mind those who find faith difficult or impossible, unreasonable and unable to carry conviction, repellent, ludicrous, a museum-piece.

How then do we start to think about faith? It is not as if we never use the word in ordinary talk. We profess to have faith in so-and-so's judgement, or to have faith in new remedies for ailments or in travel-agents or builders who can be relied upon to deliver the goods, or in the policies of a political party. The resonances which such utterances and opinions carry are not our concern at this point. *Here* we need to make clear that the faith which is here intended is faith in *God.* Faith as expressed in the sort of everyday instances which we have just mentioned causes us no problems. In each and all of them we will have grounds available for establishing whether or not our faith was justified – so-and-so's judgement can itself be assessed and verified, the remedies will be found either to work or to fail to work, the travel-agents and builders can be judged by results, likewise (given a slightly longer time-scale) the policies of the political party. But faith in God is a different matter. The heart of it is expressed succinctly by the New Testament writer who said 'anyone who comes to God must believe that he exists.' When we try to think about faith *in God,* we move into a different dimension. We move from the realm of *what is* to the realm of *what may be,* from the verifiable to the unverifiable, from the predictable to the speculative.

But are we ready to speak of *God?* Does the mere mention of *God* not cloud the issue with presuppositions? Do not let us at this stage speak too easily of God. If it is true that "God" is 'the most loaded of all human words', and that it has been soiled with misuse, the longer we can continue the discussion without resort to that particular term, the more likely we are to be heard. Those who do have faith in God must take seriously and sensitively that for countless persons the idea of faith in God, certainly in any institutionalised expression of it, is actually and actively repellent. It is to them much as one of those hideous and lifeless white marble altars which disfigure so many continental churches, decked with artificial flowers and faded lace and often flanked on the walls by vapid and insipid representations of the Sacred Heart of Jesus or of St. Teresa of Avila (in truth the least vapid and insipid of women). It is removed from the warm, flesh-and-blood, life of the real world. It smells of ecclesiasticism, of musty hymn-books and of an unwarranted and artificial constriction of the wide, generous horizons of authentic living. It is devoid of life and dynamism. It is irrelevant.

If then we are not yet to speak of God, in what terms shall we think so that the discussion can go forward? If we cannot find such terms, the discussion does not deserve to go forward;

for we shall be implying that no rational discourse can take place, since the key concept is in a form which can only be uttered, not analysed, discussed or given alternative expression. But we want the discussion to go forward, or else we should not be engaging in it by reading what is written. So what sort of terms, what sort of language shall we employ? To answer that question, we must ask another. What *sort of question* are we asking when we ask about faith? We are asking – is there a fundamental and final reality which underlies, goes beyond and is responsible for all that is? Is there a goal for all that exists? Does existence have aim and purpose and therefore hope? Is the fundamental and final reality such that we can *entrust* ourselves to it? We are not asking questions about who there may be up in the sky but about the innermost and ultimate nature of all that *is,* including the question why *anything is* at all (why is there *something* and not *nothing*?). We are asking questions about *ourselves,* about the thoughts of our heads and the desires of our hearts, about what meaning and significance these may have and to what they may point.

This matter of terms, of *language,* is of great importance. In marriage-relationships, it sometimes comes about that an impasse is reached because, as is said, husband and wife no longer speak to each other with any meaning, no longer communicate, i.e. have no means of communion with each other. Part at least of the causation of this can be found in the conditioned responses which each makes to the other, so that the language they use no longer carries a valid message but serves only to signal a predictable feeling which in turn evokes a corresponding reaction. So, if the relationship is to have new life and hope breathed into it, a new language has to be found, one which does not automatically carry in itself all the hackle-raising and despair-inducing potential of the old language. The search for a new and liberating language is of great significance, and of no little difficulty, in human relationships, calling for much determination, perseverance and commitment. Those who value their relationships, in particular their marriage and all that is contained in it, are prepared to provide such commitment, rightly judging the cause to be uniquely worth-while. All this mirrors with almost unnerving clarity the state of our relationship with whatever ultimate reality there may

be and of the language in which it is expressed. Because the
language has, for many persons, gone stale and tired and
become overloaded with negative signals, the relationship itself
has in many instances been deemed to be untenable or
non-existent. Because it can no longer be pursued credibly
within the framework of the old language, it has been deemed
to be no longer pursuable *at all*. Because no alternative language
has been offered, beyond any which they may privately invent,
the question of faith has for many become virtually unthinkable
and undiscussible.

So we must be prepared to use language which for many will
be new, though it has been the coinage of philosophers for long
enough. For a while a least it will be helpful to keep to the
negative path over language and also to speak more about
ourselves than straightaway about any ultimate reality
describable in personal or supra-personal terms. We may reflect
whether we are in fact prepared to declare the universe a
meaningless place, a place of chance and pure hazard, without
purpose or goal, without hope or hope of any hope. Do we
recognise ourselves as undeclared nihilists? It is possible to
come to such a position almost by default, without realising
the full implications which a denial of faith can hold. 'To the
nihilist it is the totality which is suspect; reality as a whole and
especially his own life seem to him profoundly unstable, fragile
and ephemeral: fleeting, empty, ineffective, discordant, in the
last resort useless, pointless, worthless – in a word, null.' So Hans
Küng paints the cold night of nihilism.[1] It is a position of
unrelenting harshness. It is the logical outcome of thorough-
going atheism. Yet it is not a conviction to which many could
happily subscribe in a full-blooded and deliberate way, and most
would be horrified if it was thought of as representing their
outlook. Most of us are in fact *not* prepared to declare the
universe, and our own lives within it, meaningless, empty, void
and null. Such a declaration is a long way from representing
the convictions which actually inform and energize our lives,
all the stronger for being in most cases unarticulated. The
practices of our living reflect unrecognised convictions.

If then it is true that many persons would recoil from the
position implied by their half-thought assumptions of the
impossibility of faith, we may enquire how this comes about.

Language which has become tired, irrelevant and repellent undoubtedly plays its part in producing misconceptions. But language, terminology, cannot bear the whole burden. We need to look wider afield. We need to ask what are the characteristics of today's world which lead so many persons to *assume* that faith is not a valid option. For it is observably true that many – perhaps the great majority of persons – live today not upon principles derived from a convinced position of belief or unbelief, faith or denial of faith, but in the half-light of assumptions derived by a sort of osmosis from the working conventions of the world and society around them. If we consider the nature of those conventions, prime amongst them must be *an uncritical acceptance of the need for the demonstrability of all knowledge which claims to be authentic*. We imagine that we derive this view from the methods of natural science, but in fact knowledge of this kind is to be found in only one field, that of mathematics. Mathematics, until it is applied, is in itself a purely theoretical science, a science of pure logic. Once it moves outside its own theoretical realm and becomes applied, it becomes also open to all the contingencies which belong to the real world. Mathematics is a noble science and of incalculable value, but it is not a guide to the way in which we actually think in the real world, nor does it demonstrate the kind of reasoning to which the real world must be susceptible if it is to yield evidence of the possibility of meaning and purpose.

But whilst the mathematical method lurks in our minds as an unconscious assumption about the means and method of all true and trustworthy knowledge, more formative still are the practical appurtenances of our technological age. What should be taken as the typical sound of our modern world? The shriek of the high-speed train, the clash and clank and rattle of a car production-line? Is it not rather the electronic bleep and the clack of the computer keys? Very few modern processes do not now involve computers. They are omnipresent. They give us answers based on data of ever-increasing complexity. They take a diversity of factors and give us a prediction, telling us the best line for the new motorway and the best moment to sell our shares, the best concentration of tank fire-power and the setting needed for a smart bomb to reach its target. They get spacecraft into space and back to earth. At the other end of the timescale they help us to date archaeological finds with startling accuracy. They are the means of a vast range of instant knowledge and of achievement based upon it. They need an ever growing army to write their programmes, a highly-skilled (and therefore highly-paid) occupation. They are instruments, technical aids to learning and to a host of practical endeavours. But because it is difficult to use something habitually and not to be in any degree influenced by it, they make their contribution to the assumptions of our time, to the prevailing mental climate. The sheer availability of so great a volume of information at the touch of a few keys does its part in promoting the assumption (uncriticised and unconscious like all assumptions) that what is most real and significant is what can be summoned up in this way. Moreover, and importantly, computers are a refined component in that aspect of today's thinking which militates against risks and the taking of risks – the emphasis on prediction and planning on 'feeding it all into the computer', the 'percentage basis', risk-limitation. (There is even an option in golf for the 'percentage shot'!) All this is against the idea of self-venturing. It does not make for a milieu which is favourable and encouraging to the invitation of faith to venture ourselves.

The character of today's typical mental climate, as drawn in this brief and selective sketch can be aptly illustrated by what Feuerbach wrote in the last century: 'Christianity has in fact long vanished not only from the reason but from the life of mankind, so that it is nothing more than a *fixed idea*, in flagrant contradicton with our fire and life assurance companies, our railroads and steam-carriages, our picture and sculpture galleries, our military and industrial schools, our theatres and scientific museums.'[2] The deliciously quaint and dated character of those words should not disguise that they still summarise much of our general feeling about the impropriety of faith in the setting of today's world. How then does faith make reply?

We may start by pointing out that, as we have already suggested, for many persons what they do and what they are prepared explicitly to believe are at odds with each other. Most persons do not understand the implications for faith of many of their ways of acting and deciding. Faced with a total reality, a universe, which is in itself uncertain and ambiguous, we do yet act for the most part in ways which exhibit a fundamental trust in it as having meaning and purpose. That is to say, we act in ways which denote a basic attitude which is at the opposite pole from nihilism. This acting is so instinctive and uncriticised that we fail to notice its significance, let alone pay heed to its implications for discovering what we believe. Nevertheless all our planning and hoping, all our humanitarian causes, all our concern with self-fulfilment, all these imply a basic attitude of trust towards the total reality which both confronts us and of which we are part. Nor is the truth of this basic attitude greatly affected by the particularities of our temperament. As we shall have cause to observe, some temperaments are more trusting than others. But such differences do not decide more than the details of our acting. The overall pattern and sweep of what we do and of the value which we place upon it exhibits an attitude which is basically trusting of total reality, ambiguous as the reality is.

Intuitively and unconsciously trusting we may be, as implied by the total pattern of our actions. Nevertheless, our normal conscious assumption is that we do things, take all important decisions, rationally, as the result of an unbroken chain of reasoning. When we are faced with the possibility of faith, we realise sharply that no such chain of reasoning can carry us to faith. Here we move into the need to consider two questions: first, what function, if any, reason has in relation to faith; second, what actual function reason and rationality discharge in our own lives. Whilst these two questions are related, it will be seen that they are of different kinds. The first is a matter of principle, more general, more 'philosophical', the second a matter of observation and discernment.

To say that reason has *nothing* to do with faith would be monstrous. It would rightly earn the contempt of all except fundamentalist fideists, those who by definition believe that faith has no place for the operation of reason. For our intellect, by which we exercise reason and rationality, is a precious and definitive part of ourselves, a crucial sign of our identity as humans. To propose that we should, or could, as it were leave it outside the door, would be to say that this dominant and

distinctive faculty has no part nor lot with the matter of
faith. That could not be, since it would entail resigning or
suppressing a vitally distinguishing capacity in ourselves. If faith
is to be a true and authentic commitment of ourselves, then
it will be of our *entire* selves, not of some believing or 'religious'
part of ourselves in separation from the rest of us. Our intellect,
our reason, must have full and unfettered play, *and must expect
to continue to do so.* But at the same time, the exercise of reason
alone cannot bring us to faith. Total reality, uncertain and
ambiguous as it is, is not susceptible to reason to compel it
to reveal the truth of its being. There can be no *proof* of its
having meaning and purpose, such as will relieve us of all
further seeking. Here a misleading complication has been
introduced by former talk of 'proofs of the existence of God'
within certain traditions of the Church, misleading because no
such proof, in any normal sense of the term, can exist. There
is, of course, that within us which wistfully hankers after
proof, but as we may comfort ourselves that if some such
'proof' were claimed, it would prove nothing which had to do
with any total and underlying reality that may be. Yet, such
'proof' apart, our rational capacity has a crucial role to play.
Perhaps *in itself* it cannot bring us even to the verge of faith,
but its continued functioning with regard to the meaning of
a faith which has been found is unconditionally necessary.

But how far are we rational beings, and how far are our main
decisions rational ones? Falling in love, choosing a house,
changing our work, choosing a particular educational path for
our children – how far are such decisions as these taken
purely on grounds of reason? We are not attempting to imply
that all decisions which are not *purely* rational (i.e. arrived at
purely by a logical chain of reasoning) are thereby *irrational*.
We are enquiring, rather: what is the relationship of reason
to our total decision? When we fall in love, the heart, our
affections, will have the commanding say, and may succeed in
subduing reason into a very subordinate position. Nevertheless,
we should not thereby be prevented from giving a rational
account of the affair nor will reason have played no part at all,
however unconscious of it we may have been. When we choose
a house, there is a host of factors which reason will take into
account, the number of rooms, the heating, the garden, the

price, the location and so on. But these alone will not decide whether or not we purchase that house. It must, overall, be a house in which we can envisage feeling happy and at home. It must in some way accord with ourselves. There will have to be a weighing of objective and subjective factors, and the latter will certainly punch their full weight. If we consider changing our job, moving from one profession to another completely different one, e.g. leaving industry for teaching, we shall certainly have to take rational account of such matters as relative rates of pay, relative prospects for us in each of the professions, the state and stage of our family, as well as the more personal and subjective factors of how we feel about our existing work, what wishes and hopes we find stirring within us. We may find ourselves faced with a balance of disparate factors, and the reaching of a decision will be difficult, even beset with agony of mind and heart, probing us to our depths. In the end we shall decide, not wholly on the grounds of reason, but because we shall have reached an 'existential moment' in which the matter will have become clear. Much the same sort of procedure will be followed in reaching some of the desperately balanced decisions which many people have to reach concerning their children's education.

What have these typical examples of main decisions shown? In each and all of them reason has played a greater or lesser role, in one guise or another. None of the decisions was irrational, but neither was it *wholly rational* as if reached by the exercise of a pure and disembodied reason. No simple assessment of advantages and disadvantages, pros and cons, could enable us to reach a decision without further ado, though such assessment had an important role to play. In the end we had to *decide*, hoping that our choice was right, having done our best to evaluate all the factors and feelings. Nothing outside ourselves, no accumulation of factors, could take the decision for us. We had to put ourselves, head, heart and all into the decision and take it. And very quickly the decision would demonstrate itself to us as right or wrong. Each of these decisions resulted in something which had thereafter to be lived with and lived *in*. Each of them in varying fashion involved the whole of ourselves. Each decision was reached by an exercise of our rational capacity within the setting of our total selves, not apart from ourselves, as if the rest of our being had no part to play.

Does what we have observed of some typical human decisions and the nature of our involvement in reaching them throw any light upon the nature of our decision for or against faith? We may remind ourselves that by *faith* we are signifying faith in an underlying and final reality, responsible for all that is and giving to all that is a meaning and a goal. It will be certainly safe to say that, if the kinds of decision which we have sketched are difficult to reach, the decision concerning faith will in some ways be infinitely more so. But perhaps we shall find the primary difficulty to lie in realising that there is a decision to be made at all; and only then encounter the difficulty of reaching the decision in ways which are identical with the ways of reaching our here-and-now decisions about marriage, housing, jobs and education. For in those examples we saw that when all has been balanced up in a rational manner, there comes the 'existential moment' of decision, which involves much more of us than simply our faculty of reason. Will this not be much more the case when the matter for decision involves the totality of ourselves? Just as in the process of falling in love or deciding to buy a particular house we move almost imperceptibly from rational assessment to something far more inclusive of our whole selves, so when we are faced with the deepest question of truth which confronts any person in this world will this not be a fortiori the case? The deeper and more totally embracing the truth, the greater will be our uncertainty about it on grounds of pure reason, and the greater part, inevitably, will be played by the existential factors involved in every decision of human consequence.

What will summon us to make the venture of faith, to move to that moment when we understand that more is involved of ourselves than simply our intellect and reason? We shall examine this more closely in a later chapter. Here let us simply observe that we have referred to the *venture of faith*. That phrase is vividly re-expressed by the words of a Russian theologian: 'The existence of God is known by an act of madness, daring and love; it is to throw the thread of life into the heavens in the certainty that it will take hold there without any guarantee of causality; it is a dumb, beseeching act; it is a prayer[3]. However it may appear in each individual case, with whatever actual circumstances and subjective sense it may come clothed, that is the reality about faith, faith in God. It involves reason, but reason alone can never achieve it. Part of what faces any person who contemplates faith in God lies in accepting that.

[1]*Does God Exist?*, p. 149.
[2]L. Feuerbach, *Wesen des Christentums,* pp. 29-30 (Quoted in H. Küng, *Does God Exist?,* p. 208).
[3]E. Lampert, *The Divine Realm,* p. 43.

CHAPTER 2

What Kind of God?

'The most loaded of all human words'. Near the beginning of the previous chapter we quoted that assessment of the word, term, or title 'God'. With that in mind we carried on our discussion largely without using it, having suggested certain phrases as a working substitute. We referred to 'a fundamental and final reality which underlies, goes beyond and is responsible for all that is'. Even such phraseology, as neutral as possible, making no concessions to explicitly religious terms or conceptions, carries with it certain implications. Do not the words 'responsible for' themselves suggest some idea of the personal, even a person? Since that implication alone is sufficient to raise plenty of questions it is clear that we cannot go further without some discussion of what is necessarily contained in the idea of God.

We could start by remarking that there is something outrageous, bizarre and monstrous in *discussing* God, even though that has been happening in one form or another since human speech began and will continue until such speech falls silent. That observation is a way of starting to draw attention to what must necessarily be present in any conception of God which is worth discussion. If God is to be indeed God, he must be the source of all that is and the goal of all that is, the uncaused, the infinite and unconditioned. He cannot be derived from 'elsewhere', or that 'elsewhere' would be God. Some words of Hans Küng may illuminate our thinking about this aspect of God: 'Believing in the Creator of the world means affirming in enlightened trust that the world and man do not remain inexplicable in their ultimate source, that the world and man are not pointlessly hurled from nothing into nothing, but that in their totality they are meaningful and valuable, not chaos but cosmos'.[1] Certainly the God of whom we speak cannot be less than that, which places ourselves in the relationship of created to creator, so that all we are and may become, every hope and every particle of meaning which we may claim

16

to possess, comes from him and goes to him. For us to discuss him therefore contains ipso facto an element of the monstrous and bizarre, since if God is God, only worship, not discussion, is appropriate. Yet at the same time our discussing God, and our ability to do so, have a quite different implication, and one of fundamental importance. They are a sign of our freedom. God does not force himself upon us, but leaves us free. Freedom and faith are correlative to each other, just as freedom and faith are correlative to the hiddenness of God. For, if God is indeed God, his unveiled presence would annihilate our freedom and overwhelm us utterly. Whatever else is to be said, it is certain that mortal man is not made to stand in the unmediated presence of God.

But God is not present in unmediated form, though sometimes in our ignorance and foolishness we all but wish that he were. If God is God, he is present hidden and veiled. All the world of phenomena, all the myriad myriads of varied visibles which compose the universe, these are the veil of God. But if that is indeed the truth, is God then a person, in some fashion *outside* this vast and mysterious scene of all that exists, making himself an addition to it? If we have difficulty in conceiving such a possibility, we are right. If God is God, he is not *a* person, however exalted and magnified. To speak of God as personal, or supra-personal, *more* than personal, is indeed to speak of him in the only terms which could bear credence. We cannot, and must not, think of a God who is in any way *less* than ourselves, *less* than personal – that is to lapse into utter meaninglessness. But to speak of God as personal is not to speak of him as *a person*. To conceive of him as *a person* is to make him one of a series, however we qualify the conception. Similarly, if we change the language and speak of him as *a* being, then we still make him one of a class. For God cannot be *an* anything. If he exists, he is *Being itself,* the source of all *being,* particularised and manifested in *beings.* Similarly he cannot be *located, here* rather than *there.* He must be equally present in all times and in all places. He is therefore not removed from, and outside, our world and the universe of which it is part. He is *in* it, giving it his own life, supporting and energising it from moment to moment in a seamless sequence of time.

All this is the spelling out of a tiny part of what it means for God to be God; the confrontation of ourselves by this unspeakable mystery in which, if it is truth, lies the whole meaning and possibility of our life. If we have removed one serious obstacle to belief, in the form of the idea that God is *a person,* then the discussion so far has not been in vain. At least we have moved into an area in which the light which illuminates the true nature of the faith-decision has been brightened a little, a few dark windows of misconception prevented from continuing to block the passage of such light. But our discussion so far has remained confined to thinking about what is *necessary* to any conception of God which claims to be valid. We have exercised our power of reason, and, we may believe, to good effect. But now we must let ourselves be confronted by the claim of the *divine initiative.* God, as we have seen, is hidden and veiled by the totality of existence, that which, if he is God, is his creation. But the claim of *Christian* faith is that God has unveiled himself, *revealed* himself in the person, life, death and resurrection of the man Jesus. Here some justification must be offered for speaking of God's revelation of himself specifically in terms of this having occurred in Jesus (*Christian* faith because it is faith in Jesus as the *Christ, Messiah, anointed one,* of God). We speak with such specific reference because Christian faith is the prevailing faith of the Western world, because the readers of this book will be likely to have been reared in this faith, if in any. It is not in neglect or belittlement of other world faiths, though it is also wise not to minimise the profound differences which exist between Christian faith and other faiths (a difference which one can easily verify in a concrete manner by attending an inter-faith service). It behoves us to be aware of the positive, and often corrective, insights, of the other world-religions, even if we are ourselves committed to faith in Jesus Christ as the revealer of God. Christians may, and do, believe that God's revealing of himself in Jesus was definitive and authentic, but that does not carry with it the consequences that they should reckon other faiths as of no account and of no truth-content. There are profound truths about the world and our treatment of it upon which the grasp of other religions is at times firmer and more perceptive than the Christian tradition.

What are the implications of the concept of *God's initiative* for faith? If Jesus indeed carries this initiative in himself, we must also say that it is in a mode which is utterly consistent with the hiddenness of God behind the veil of all that exists. He does not come with fanfares of trumpets, but is born quietly into an obscure corner of the world, a corner distinguished only by the faith of its people in a supreme and sole God. In his brief time of public life he gathers a small company round him, heals some persons in a way which, though remarkable, was not unparalleled or inexplicable, teaches with piercing originality but provoking the religious leaders into regarding him as the maker of dangerous and blasphemous claims, endures a specious trial, suffers death by being impaled on a wooden cross, is entombed and then – *what?* The small company of close friends and followers whom he had collected round himself became convinced that he was alive. Their first conviction spread. The Church was born. This is as brief and factual account as can be given of the birth, life, ministry, death and being alive again of Jesus. The crucial aspect of it all for *faith* is that at no point in the whole 'process' of Jesus is anything done which might subtract from the freedom which constitutes the only authentic operational setting of faith. If Jesus uniquely expresses God in the existence of an utterly human life, it is so done that at no juncture is there any less demand for faith. The response to Jesus of those whom he first invited to go with him was a response of trust, and the response has been of the same kind ever since.

But was the resurrection of Jesus not an exception to this? Was the resurrection not an act of supernatural power, which left no choice but to believe? It will not have escaped notice that, when the whole process and progress of Jesus was being summarily described, the term *'resurrection'* was not used. To say that the resurrection *'happened'* is to make the same sort of mistake as to refer to God as *a person.* Just as God cannot be described as *a person,* one, however exalted an one, of a class to which others belong, so the resurrection cannot be described as having *happened* in a way which would render it an event, a member, however exceptional, of a class which has innumerable other members in the form of events. The resurrection is not part of an historical series, even though it

was within history that the friends of Jesus became aware of
his aliveness and continue to do so to this day. To speak in this
way in no degree impugns the narrative of the resurrection of
Jesus in the Gospels. The aliveness of Jesus could be told *in
no other way.* The writers of the Gospels, who had produced their
inspired narratives to proclaim their faith in Jesus as an
unique human expression of God – and more than that ('Son
of God') – could not at the all-important point abandon that
form, nor did they command the thought-categories with
which to do so, had they even wanted to. The indescribable
can by definition, only be symbolically represented; and the
resurrection stories of the Gospels, not least the oldest and
shortest of them, that of St. Mark, are the most precious
symbolic representations of the totally indescribable truth that
Jesus had passed from death to life. He had died the death that
confronts every one born into this world, and which outsoars
all other 'problems', being the problem of our life having
meaning or not; he had died this *hope-denying* death and through
it had become reunited with the life of the underlying and final
reality which we call God. 'Resurrection therefore means
positively that Jesus did not die into nothingness, but in
death and from death died into that incomprehensible and
comprehensive absolutely last/absolutely first reality, was
indeed taken up by that most real reality, which we designate
by the name of God. And it is this very fact that the first
witnesses regard as having universal importance, as having also
importance for me.'[2] The importance of those words lies both
in their fresh casting of the truth of the resurrection and also
of the explicit expression of that truth in terms which are those
which we employed when thinking about what is necessary to
any concept of God which could claim to be valid. In so far
as there is some fresh language here, introduced into our
thinking about that point upon which the truth of the whole
Christian claim about Jesus must rest, this may have helped
in giving new life and possibility to what had grown tired and
unreal. When there is a new language, it is not so easy to make
our conditioned responses, nor indeed so tempting to do so.

   The problem of faith, the need for faith, of course remains,
for the good reason that there is no alternative. Earlier we saw
that the exercise of reason by itself can never bring us to faith.

But the more authentic and comprehensive the material upon which our reason may reflect, the more clearly and authentically will the real choice which confronts us appear. So often mythology and misconceptions distort the true nature of the material upon which the decision of faith must be made. But the *need* for that decision is never taken from us. After all, it is the hall-mark of our freedom, the sign of our authentic humanity. But, when that is said, *how* do we come to faith? At least, if the main position of this chapter bears weight, we shall be deciding about the commitment of faith not in a distant God, but in a God who has drawn utterly near and remains for ever closer to us than ourselves.

[1] H. Küng, *Does God Exist?*, p. 641.
[2] H. Küng, *Does God Exist?*, p. 679.

CHAPTER 3

Coming to Faith

The late Archbishop Michael Ramsey was a great man of God and a great human being. His immense intellect was the servant of his faith and he was in himself, as are all persons of true holiness, a living argument for God. Speaking once on television about prayer, he stared confidingly out of the screen and said simply 'Be yourself: be yourself.' There are many who have spent much of their lifetime searching for their true selves who would hear this as a counsel of perfection. Nevertheless, the point remains. If you want to embark upon an adventure in an authentic manner, start from what you know best; start with yourself.

But that proposal – start with yourself – will have an alien, even unwelcome sound in some ears. Awareness of ourselves is for some people unhealthy, with words such as 'intro-spective' hung around it. There is a positive disinclination to do anything deliberate in the way of thinking about ourselves, as opposed to thinking about our own interests, how to make the next twenty-five thousand (or million) pounds, sell a property, take over a company, pass the next lot of exams, pay the school fees, keep the family clothed and fed, get a part-time job or sail a boat. We often regard ourselves – not entirely without justification – as something of a can of worms on which the lid had better be kept firmly fastened. But whilst this attitude or feeling is understandable, it cannot in truth be encouraged or defended. We have only one life, and we are our own most precious asset, even if it is true that we are sometimes also our own greatest liability. If that is so, there are self-evident grounds for saying that we ought not to neglect this asset, but should pay attention to it in all its aspects. We should have concern not only for our physical health, with all our mania for fitness and health clubs, but for the health of our less visible and tangible but even more real selves – our mental and psychic and (if the term may be allowed) spiritual selves.

If we tend to plot against paying heed to ourselves, we certainly have many fellow-conspirators to aid and abet us. The world in general seems to conspire in a gigantic confidence-trick, to con us into placing a far greater value upon *doing* than upon *being*. It is easy to see how this comes about, and why we so frequently fall for it. The world, society, needs the endless range of skilled activity which men and women can offer. Day after day, in every conceivable corner of the world, enterprises are carried forward, lives made tolerable, safety and security ensured, knowledge imparted, conceptions translated into tangible realities, through the exercise of the practical talents of human beings, many of which require enormous expenditure of planning and thoughtfulness in their deployment. By the exercise of such talents both the life of the world community is carried on and men and women express themselves and gain fulfilment. All of that needs to be said firmly and positively, though it is evident and well known. It is less evident and well known to the great majority of persons, that the tale of these practical abilities does not take account of the entirety of ourselves by any means. In fact there is an inmost part of ourselves, a centre and depth to us, of which it takes account only incidentally and haphazardly. What we are talking about is ourselves *as* ourselves, *in* ourselves and *for* ourselves – ourselves as beings, precious, unique and unrepeatable.

It is also part of the conspiracy brought about by modern patterns of living that we shall not have time to be silent and to take stock. But standing still, being silent and taking stock, are crucial means of our becoming authentically human, full and mature persons. Without them large parts of ourselves never realise their potential, and such unliberated and unrealised aspects can in due course often cause us major and mystifying difficulty. We must take our *being* seriously, as something to be loved and nurtured. To allow ourselves times of reflection upon our feelings and hopes is not luxury but radical and fundamental necessity. Only when we allow ourselves such opportunities will the major questions arise in our minds. What do I want? What is the world like, and what is my place in it? Am I committed to anything with the whole of my being? What indeed is 'the whole of my being', and do

I have much conception of myself as an entire person? Where
is my trust? Do I in fact entrust myself to anything? These are
searching and probing questions, and for that reason we
frequently leave them unasked. But obscure and difficult as the
answers to them may be, they nevertheless are the questions
which lay us open to reality and to new depths of living.

Perhaps that last sentence provides the clue as to why we
should start with ourselves in the approach to faith. For faith
is not a matter of a series of propositions which we must
assent to with our head, a purely cerebral act without the
involvement of the whole of ourselves. However, we are not
attuned, or only haphazardly, to the deliberate and embracing
involvement of our whole and deepest selves. The primary need
is to *collect* ourselves, to realise ourselves, to lay hold upon our
being in its entirety. By this existential realisation of ourselves
we shall have started to combat that danger of being a one-
dimensional person, a danger much at hand in the world of
our time. In this realisation of ourselves as an entire person
every faculty and aspect of ourselves will be engaged, emotion
and will, feeling and instinct, mind and body, head and heart,
our objectivity and our subjectivity, the known and the
unknown, the open and the mysterious in ourselves, our
conscious and our unconscious. If faith is for life and for
living, the decision for faith must involve all these elements
in ourselves, all these aspects which cohere in the one total,
organic person. By the conscious effort to collect and realise
ourselves we shall make faith more possible, since authentic
faith belongs to the whole person and illuminates the whole
person.

To what may we compare the one who is approaching faith?
Here we are not at present speaking of those in the abnormal
circumstances of crisis or breakdown, but in a setting more akin
to normality. Perhaps we may compare him or her more to an
angler casting a line out into a river than to a mathematician
working at his desk upon a problem. For the angler is overtly
in *action*. With each cast of his line he commits something of
himself, and something of his hopes. His whole action is an
action of hope, a finding out whether there is anything there
waiting and willing to respond to his cast. He may cast, skillfully
and commitedly, for hour after hour and evoke nothing, no

sign of interest, no stirring of the waters, nothing on the end of his line – 'we have toiled all the night and taken nothing.' And then, with a cast identical with all the others he has made through the hours, something is *there*, to his relief and delight and surprise. *There* is something of life and movement, when he was starting to doubt whether there was anything other than water, *there* is the tug and the pull, the actuality of something of being and living, positive and strong.

This contains strong pointers for what is involved in coming to faith. There must be *action*, resulting from a decision. There is something of *doing* demanded, and at times actual practical action may be called for – asking and investigating, going and seeing. But the action will be in the first place an inward movement, and inward willingness to start on a journey, uncertain where it will finish, but a willingness to commit oneself to *going* and therefore *changing* ('I will arise and go to my father'.)

But *what* will move us, induce us, persuade us, encourage us, provoke us, to *make the movement*, to cast the line? Do not let us be deceived: once we have *made the movement, cast our line*, we have started to come to faith, and we shall discover that, by a sudden reversal, *we* are on the end of the line and being hauled in by God. But *what will move us*? Let us not be afraid to say that here we enter a realm of considerable mystery. What elements go into the chemistry will be subtly different in each case, for each of us is unique, and the being of each is a vital and major element, one decisive factor, in the total chemistry of the coming to faith. There is no standard pattern, for there are no standard persons. But there may be an event, some happening, which disturbs and stirs the existing pattern and assumptions of our existence. An accident, a bereavement, a loss of employment, even a national or international catastrophe, may be amongst the happenings which probe and stir us and set us in motion. More frequently the causation may be more domestic – the timely word of a friend or priest, a broadcast, some words chanced upon in the Bible, an encounter with a holy place or person, questions posed by our children, or a gathering cumulative sense in ourselves that there is more to existence than we have yet discovered, a disturbing appre-hension of inadequacy and need, a dissatisfaction with the explanations offered by the generally accepted chain of cause and effect. If we are to 'rise' from the near-mesmeric enslavement stemming from the acceptance of such a chain of cause and effect and all that it symbolises to a conviction of the infinite and primal ground of all being as 'personal', that is a conviction of God, the energy and motivation must come from within ourselves. There must be an act of rebellion, an existential outcry from deep within ourselves that we do not belong to a world of determinist cause and effect but to a world which ultimately has meaning and freedom.

The decision to cast our line into the waters to find whether it will take hold and bring faith to us is the most profound and life-embracing decision that any man or woman, boy or girl – let us not rule out the amazing faith of some of the young – can take. And it is a decision which we must all take *and indeed do take.* Contrary to much supposition, it cannot go by default and fail to be taken ('that the question be not put'). *Not* to decide about faith, to drift on without decision, is in fact to decide against faith, against the possibility of it; and such a decision may in many cases be inconsistent with what is implied by some of our practical attitudes. There is no avoidance of the decision. But it must be a *real* decision, real to ourselves, expressive of our integrity. We have seen earlier how new language is needed when the old has grown tired, distant and repellent. We need language which does not ask us to go too far too fast, to subscribe to more than we are able. We need language which liberates and does not constrict or tie us down in a way for which we are not ready. We need language which both challenges and cheers. Is not the entry of Dag Hammarskjöld, Secretary-General of the United Nations until his tragic death in 1961, in his diary for Pentecost of that year, a classic statement in such language? 'I don't know Who – or what – put the question, I don't know when it was put, I don't even remember answering. But at some moment I did say Yes to Someone – or Something – and from that hour I was certain that existence is meaningful and that, therefore, my life, in self-surrender, had a goal.' There could be no more authentic words for our time to describe coming to faith.

CHAPTER 4

The Community of Faith

Very little of what has been said so far has implied that
persons are other than separate individuals. We have spoken
about the effect of society's assumptions and thought-forms
upon their thinking, but in themselves and for themselves they
have so far remained isolated in their individuality. This
has been deliberate. We cannot forever shelter behind the
corporate, behind groupings, of whatever kind, and thereby
evade the responsibility which belongs to each of us in our
human personhood. We do not promote our own dignity
nor enhance the stature of our being by playing down this
unique responsibility for ourself which each of us has. The
responsibility for each other on which we rightly lay stress does
not take away from the responsibility of each of us for *our* self.

When that is said, it is nevertheless true that there is no
authentic human life which is not lived in relationship and
thereby becomes a shared life. There are tragic exceptions which
illuminate the normality of the general rule – those beset with
autism, who live in a non-communicating world of their own,
those temporarily or permanently placed at a great distance
from relationship with others by a severe psychotic condition.
People can place themselves in physical isolation for periods
of time – those conducting experiments or undertaking
polar exploration, for example, without in the slightest way
affecting the truth of our character as *social* beings, those who
instinctively associate with each other. Of course some persons
are by temperament and inclination more sociable than others,
whilst at the far end of the scale are those who are sometimes
referred to by others as 'natural solitaries'. But just as we saw
earlier on that the relative trustingness or untrustingness of
particular individual natures does not affect the overall
character of human action as exhibiting practical trust in the
total sum of reality as meaningful, so the comparative sociability
or unsociability of individual persons does not affect the

truth of human nature as fundamentally social. We realise ourselves fully in relationships, we grow and develop through relationships, we come to know ourselves through relationships, we express ourselves through relationships. All these are substantial contributions to the total being of ourselves as *persons* and not as social solipsisms, one-dimensional objects. In a true sense, therefore, any discussion of persons which fails to take account sooner or later of their relational nature is moving in the realm of the abstract. So far we have not so taken account, but now we can no longer desist from it.

There was a moment in the last chapter, when enquiry was made as to what might cause any man or woman to make the movement towards faith, and amongst possible causes no mention was made of contact with the *community of faith*. Such an idea could not be mentioned as just one amongst others. For the community of faith is so inclusive a concept, so fundamental to the gift and life of faith that it demands treatment for itself and in itself. It is the whole matter of the entire dimension of faith which we call social or shared. If in fact we do ask the question again – what are the things which might cause anyone to make the movement towards faith, to cast their line out into the waters? – we are in truth most likely to mention fairly soon *contact with the community of faith*.

Here we must once more pay heed to the question of language. Earlier on we discussed the habit which language possesses of growing tired, misused, empty and repellent, failing thereby to do the work which it once did effectively. We tried therefore to speak more in terms of the underlying and final reality than to use the word 'God', since so many false associations have become attached to it. We can no longer expect that the mere utterance of a single word will summon up automatically and to every mind all that it truly stands for, more particularly when we are dealing with 'the most loaded of all human words'. We can no longer be oblivious of the fact that such a word is so filled with negative associations as to outweigh entirely any positive content which, simply as a word, it might retain. And so it is also with *the Church*. That too has become a word from which it is now impossible to detach a host of associations, folk-memories, personal memories, primal colourings of life and thought. When any word or title has reached such a point, no amount of new description and redefinition will restore validity and credence to it. It is then time to abandon the rescue operation for a word and start to talk about the realities with which it has been associated and for which historically it has stood.

'This claim [to a knowing of God] arises as a response to a reality experienced by myself and for myself but in the context of a community and of a continuing exploration of relationship . . . Knowing God is within the church. Experiences are kindled and language learnt and developed within a community. It is clear that neither biblically nor psychologically would people be able to speak of God and come to the knowledge of him if people did not already speak about God and have the knowledge of him.' These words of David Jenkins[1] express in a vivid and penetrating way the all-important dimension of the community of faith, particularly in its role of communicating the faith by which it lives. This function of the community of faith is a common feature of every recognisable faith. There is no faith which is not shared in order that it may be known by others. Indeed, this is as we should expect. For when all the rest of our lives are marked by being shared with others, is this potential for faith alone to remain solitary and unshared, the very element which is to guide and inform all the rest? Human nature, as we have seen, is made for relationship. We do not disregard that nature and its needs when we come to faith. Indeed the faith, if it is to be a faith which accords with the inmost truth of all that is, must thereby also accord with the truth of ourselves as we are.

Do many persons find faith, in any institutionalised form, repulsive? The answer is surely, yes. But the answer becomes of significance when it leads us to ask why this should be the case. Leaving aside the ascertainable human repugnance to many forms of organised groupings, we have to ask: how far has the community of faith known itself, and does it know itself, to be that and that alone, the community of faith? Its history could be written in terms of how each of its failures, each of the ways in which it has throughout history allowed itself to be misled, has been at root a failure to recollect itself *as* the community of faith. Certainly if the community of faith is to play its full role in the kindling, living, and transmission of faith,

its perpetual first necessity is that it should understand itself
for what it is and found all its life and work upon that basis
and that alone. For whilst, no doubt, the community of faith
is *capable* of fulfilling many functions, and has historically done
so, not least in many humanitarian enterprises, in a time of
widespread rejection of faith it is healthy and provocative to
ask what it is which the community of faith can do for the world
at large *which no one else can do.* And the clear answer is that no
other body than the community of faith will explicitly and
avowedly hold the faith in God, live faith in God, teach faith
in God, communicate faith in God. That is what belongs to the
innermost nature of the community of faith, that is what
brought it to birth and kept it in life, and what must continue
to do so. But it is always those things beneath our spiritual noses
which we are most likely not to notice and so to neglect. If the
community's sense that it is the community *of faith* is not
being perpetually renewed and freshly rediscovered, then it will
become formalised and stylised in its life, lose its primal vigour
and gradually separate its faith from the realities of living. It
will develop forms of life and institution within itself which
will take their own existence unto themselves and become self-
authenticating without perpetual reference to the living, shared
life of faith in the community. To remain what it truly is,
the community *of faith,* the community must always be
commending its life to God for guidance, support, judgement,
reinvigoration and encouragement. It must do so in no token
fashion, but as the heart and marrow of what it is. It must realise
over and over and over again that its life must be given to it.
It is not a matter for its own efforts, but for its grateful and
humble acceptance. Part of the way of its rediscovering the
ground of its faith is for it to become aware that it has been
given what it could never invent or devise for itself, a quality
and depth of life and experience which is more than can be
of human making.

But is there not a danger lurking here? Is not the sort of
concern which is being sketched unhealthy in that it is self-
concerned, self-preoccupied, and self-centred? That this is not
a merely nominal danger is demonstrated by the in-turned and
over-intensive life of many of the sects. (It ought to be part of
everyone's life-experience to read Edmund Gosse's classic,

moving, and at times richly amusing, study of the early
Plymouth Brethren 'Father and Son'.) That tendency is indeed
a distortion, but serves to make plain that the danger is there.
With what are we to counter it? There are two major defences
and safeguards. The first is to keep to the mainstream of the
tradition of the community of faith, not to go off on some side-
tributary. There is a great main tradition, compounded of
doctrine, worship and spirituality, which is strong, wise,
proven and identifiable. There will always be extremist sects,
offering attractions and sometimes reminding us of aspects and
concerns which have dropped out of the mainstream; but their
faith and practice only coincide marginally with that of the
main tradition. Second, the community of faith must always
maintain full contact with the whole range of society and
be concerned for it. The implication of maintaining and
nurturing the community's life of faith is not that it should
engage in an endless process of introspection as an end in itself,
but that the living Jesus whom it is always rediscovering will
despatch it ever and anew upon his work which is the work
of God. Where the Holy Spirit of God is truly invoked and
present, he does not allow people to rest in self-concern.
Contact with the world – always living on the frontiers, as
Charles Péguy would teach us to say – keeps the community
of faith earthed, realistic, concerned for *all* people, sensitive,
alert and compassionate. The world at large must renew the
community's life as much as the other way round.

We have been speaking of the community of faith as if it were
a readily identifiable phenomenon. But is it? Is it in each and
every place a simple and easy matter to introduce anyone into
a community of faith which is recognisable as such? There are
congregations worshipping in parish churches, but are they
always communities of faith? For what is the primary hall-mark
of the community of faith in God in any place and at any time?
It is a community, a body of persons, who know that the
meaning and validity of their common life is totally dependent
upon God. They hang upon God for their meaning. They are
not looking for false certainties, or for safety policies, in fact
are looking for few certainties at all, aware that the only
certainty lies in their faith – *and that certainty itself is a fairly
strange, unusual and opaque kind of certainty.* This hanging upon

God for our meaning gives an unavoidable provisionality to affairs and to life in general, the opposite to the attitude of the man in the teaching of Jesus who built himself bigger and bigger storehouses with the proceeds of which to make himself comfortable on his equivalent to the Costa del Sol. (This provisionality is well symbolised by the Franciscan friars' insistence that none of their houses shall retain more money than is sufficient for the next three months' needs.) It gives a seeking, searching, purposeful, praying, testing, character to all important decisions. It provides a wholly different dimension within which to view all affairs, a dimension which gives risk and venture their proper role. Part of growing and developing as a community of faith comes from acting as if you were, learning to trust God in ways which in other settings might seem ill-advised. But there is more than this. A community of faith brings joy to birth in its members because it is a *community* of faith. Faith is the common possession, that which is shared together. That brings joy because it brings light, new light from God and new light upon each other. We feel that we are brought nearer to God and nearer to one another. Our shared faith becomes the most precious possession that we have.

But is that a realistic picture of the community of faith as it is found in most churches and congregations? Here we must allow for a considerable variety of idioms and expressions of faith. Certainly we could go to churches and congregations where something exhibiting the essential characteristics of the community of faith as we have sketched it out would be found. But there would be many others, and they the majority, where either the community of faith had never developed beyond a formal and stylised convention of church life or it had been persuaded to accept a counterfeit in the form of hearty conviviality. The plain truth is that in many places the community of faith has never grown into its true self because people have never really learned to encounter each other. Their only encounter has been in the setting of formal worship or in structured meetings or in smaller groups also structured and with a carefully limiting objective. Many members of apparently active, vigorous and flourishing congregations never in fact encounter each other in more than a superficial and fleeting manner. Most of them do not wish to do more than that, since they have never been encouraged to think in those terms nor been provided with the means whereby such an experience might be realised. But these are not some sort of optional extras to the life of faith. What has been said about the community of faith is absolutely basic to that life. It is the major setting in which that life is to be enabled and lived. Every congregation and its leaders must face the truth that, if there is, there is no true encounter between those who share the faith, they are not sharing it as they should and they are failing in the chief medium in which and through which that faith should be seen and known and approached by others.

Where such major deficiency exists in what ought to be the community of faith, it cannot be supplied overnight. But it is possible for much to be discovered in a short while, if the wish and the desire are there. The prerequisite is for the community to realise itself in groupings which are small and intimate enough to allow of true meeting. For that purpose most congregations require subdividing. At the outset we must get people to throw away the notion that such an exercise is for the specially devout, for those who 'go in for that sort of thing'. It is not something which demands either extraordinary piety or extraordinary powers of intellect. Nothing could be further from the truth. What *is* demanded is a commitment, a readiness to learn from others (usually one's peers), a lack of presupposition about what will emerge and a certain generosity of heart. To these needs to be united a basic expectation that, in the community of faith we will always be looking to experience new things. That is what we should expect in a community of the Holy Spirit.

So there we have a basic instrument of our discipleship within the community of faith. But where should it go from there? If groups of people are going to meet as part of the basic means of their discipleship, surely they must meet about *something*? At this point a consideration of the highest moment emerges. *Simply learning to be together as those with a common faith outweighs any other significance which the group may have.* Here is a matter which many people find initially alarming. Ought we not to have some clear and stated purpose? It may be that we *shall* discover a purpose which the group is intended by God to embrace, though we should be very searching and aware about it, not making a rush for the first possibility which appears. But the group is abundantly self-justifying simply by virtue of its members being with each other for a certain specified length of time at regular intervals. That is the over-riding reason for the group to meet together at all. Its purpose is to enable us to be with each other. That is what those who share faith ought to do. It is self-evident, once one pauses long enough to give it thought. But too frequently, apart from annual efforts like 'Lent house-groups', our congregations do not practise it. Where they do, they are witness to the deepening and enriching effect of it. Where they do not, it will require vision and leadership to bring it about.

We started to investigate the community of faith on the grounds that those who were approaching faith might well have been helped to make the movement by contact with the community, i.e. the Church in their place. If and when such a community of faith is found – and we must say that in one guise or another it often *can* be found – what may be the effects of it? We assume here that it is meeting in some such way as has been described, i.e. in a small group in a house: not more than a total of ten or twelve persons.

Prayer is the natural activity of those who have faith, so we assume that prayer will take place. It should include times of real silence, which may grow more extended as people learn to use the silence. It should not be full of set prayers. It should be uninsistent, gentle, informal, meditative. It will probably be led, but it will be *shared* prayer. The sharing is helped by the silence. In time we shall discover that silence helps to bind us closer together. The prayer is a fundamental part of the group's life. It is not because 'that is what is expected'. It is because prayer expresses us, and in prayer we grow into each other as well as into God. More properly you could say that if we grow together into God, then we grow into each other.

So – we pray: and what else? *Let that emerge.* A leader with a little experience of the life of groups can be helpful and enabling, particularly at the beginning, when courage may be at a low ebb. Learn to trust the fact of being together as those who have a common faith. Then things will start to come out. We will gain the confidence to express 'how I see things' or 'how I feel about things'. We shall learn that others have their doubts and puzzlements as well as their insights and illuminations. We shall find issues and themes which we wish to pursue. We may discover a genuine common concern and feel that God is leading us to do something about it. But more significantly, as the group continues in being, we shall discover three things. First, the group has come to have its own life, and the life matters to us, is of value to us and indeed prized by us. We start to have a sense of responsibility for it. Second, we shall find that the experience of being with those who share our faith itself strengthens that faith. To be with our fellow-believers fortifies us, not least through occasional tensions and disagreements. Third, we find a new meaning in the words 'Bear one another's burdens and so fulfil the law of Christ'. When our own faith is for any reason burning low, the faith of others, stronger at the moment, carries our own, whilst at other times ours helps to carry theirs. In this way, as in others, faith is a shared, common matter, and as such fortifies us together and gives us joy together. So we become the community of faith, a community into which others can be drawn. For, in the last analysis, faith is known only *from* community and *in* community. And part of the calling of the community of faith is to bear and carry the *unfaith* of those many who do not have faith. The few must stand before God for the many. Here is something of the true nature and vocation of the Church.

[1]D. Jenkins, *The Contradiction of Christianity*, p. 80.

CHAPTER 5

Continuing in Faith

A young man on the verge of ordination spoke to himself in something like the following terms: 'Well, you seem to have had enough faith to get you to this point, though you know very well how rocky it has been at times, and that at some moments you had no idea why you believed anything at all. But what will it be like in fifteen of twenty years time, when you are in middle-age? Will your faith have lasted you until then, and will it go on lasting?' Now the thoughts of that young man were certainly somewhat of an immature jumble but not entirely unjustifiable. It was of course very naive of him to think of faith as if it were the sand in an hour-glass – a fixed amount of it, and when it was finished, it was finished. He might have been expected to understand that faith is an organic growth, and that with proper attention and with a plentiful supply of God's grace it will grow and develop, not run out like inorganic sand. If he had been taught that, it seems that he had learned it only with the head and not with the heart also, so that it had not taken hold of him and entered into his bloodstream. But he was at least perceptive enough to see that continuing in faith is not something that can be taken for granted. If faith is indeed an organic growth, it cannot be stored up. It needs to be fed and nourished and maintained. People do lose their faith, even if they do so on grounds which are difficult to discern with any finality.

'Grant us to know that it is not the beginning of [any great enterprise] but continuing in the same until it be thoroughly finished which yieldeth the true glory.' Sir Francis Drake, that bold buccaneer, is not perhaps an obvious source of enlighten-ment on the matter of continuing in faith, but in fact his prayer discloses something of the whole character of the life of faith – continuing in the same until it be thoroughly finished. What that thorough finishing will turn out to be is not for us to say. Our concern is with the continuing. And it is the continuing which will gradually reveal the true nature of faith as we come to know it through practice.

At the outset of our being given faith in God, either as something totally new or as something reborn and revivified into more than we had ever before known, we are naturally exhilarated. And with good reason; for we have been given the most precious gift that can be given to any man or woman. We see many doors opening, a great new hope inhabiting us, and like those in Joel's prophecy we see visions and dream dreams. It is indeed exciting, and there is cause for our seeing all life *en couleur de rose*. Where before there was puzzlement and questioning, now all is assurance. We feel gloriously confident and invulnerable, and give ourselves easily and eagerly to this new life of faith. But then we find after a while that it is still possible to be assailed by doubt. It may be that something triggers it off – some setback in our work or our love-life, a disaster to a friend, the death of a loved relative, or perhaps nothing more than an utterly unrewarding time of prayer when we don't seem to get anywhere or feel anything. Whatever the precise cause, or absence of identifiable cause, God suddenly seems less certain, more distant. We feel less confident, less full of assurance. If we are honest, we will say that our feelings are negative, and we don't know how to recover our positive faith which only lately seemed so strong as to be overwhelming.

This is an important moment. It is in fact the first of a long series of such moments which will stretch throughout the length of our life of faith. Because it is the first it can be the most puzzling, and it will be helpful if there is someone at hand who can give us experienced advice. Just because it is a moment of difficulty, even of pain and distress, it is also potentially a moment of growth, *as are all such moments*. What is happening is that we are now encountering the true nature of faith and of the life of faith. We had, understandably, identified faith closely with assurance. There was good reason for us to do so. With our new-found faith came a great flood of assurance. That was natural, right and no doubt a God-sent encouragement. But faith and assurance are not one and the same. The longer we continue in the life of faith, the more cause do we find to separate them. For assurance comes and goes and there is nothing that we can do about it. Its presence is not a matter of choice or command, but is unpredictable. Insofar as this assurance is a matter of *feelings,* we need to learn that, whilst feelings are an important part of ourselves, they are not the most reliable guide to truth. Faith is *not* the equivalent of walking through life in a permanently sealed cellophane-wrapping of assurance, which nothing can remove. If that were the case, we should have outsoared the realm of faith. But that is what in this life we cannot in truth do. Faith is always the setting of life.

In the matter of continuing in faith, what does this sort of episode teach us about the real nature of faith as we know it in practice? First, we learn that in faith we have made our choice. The function of our will in relation to faith should never be belittled or despised nor should it be a matter of surprise or dismay to us, as if the will should form no part of that scene. We are not thereby painting the decision of faith as some cold-blooded affair. We know that it was not. We are saying that, in the life which follows from our decision of faith, a determined will has a proper part to play. With our will we recognise that in faith we made a choice, and that we should not depart from that choice without some overwhelming demonstration that it was false, ill-founded and mistaken. But, further than that, we come to see that *much of the experience of faith consists in feeling that we have no faith.* This is of such fundamental importance that we must look at it carefully. On the surface it appears self-contradictory. If much of the life of faith consists of feeling as if we had none, where is the distinguishing and authenticating quality of it? But the true quality of faith consists in our readiness to commit ourselves in trust *without* any felt or sensed assurance at all. The fact that such assurance very frequently does accompany our commitment to faith does not in truth affect the issue at all. It could in fact be said that the presence of any consciously felt assurance removes from faith its authentic character, however welcome in practice such assurance may be. The intrinsic nature of faith is of a bare, shorn, kind, which nevertheless has its own glory and even ultimately its own assurance. The longer we continue in the life of faith, the more we understand why this bare, unfelt, quality of faith should be as it is. And there are good reasons for this. When in Chapter

2 we were thinking about the nature of God, we thought of his hiddenness behind his creation and how we are saved from standing in his unmediated presence. God has in truth set us at an 'epistemic distance' from himself, to use John Hick's perceptive phrase, that is to say a distance not of space but of knowing and knowledge. The bareness of faith, providing ever more rarely any sensed assurance, is the way in which our actual experience corresponds to this epistemic distance.

There is, of course, a further general area from which our faith may suffer attack, namely from outside. There are always those in the world who are eager to demolish faith in God, since it is to them an offence, in the way in which we saw that Feuerbach found Christianity an offence -- 'nothing more than a *fixed idea,* in flagrant contradiction with our fire and life assurance companies, our railroads and steam carriages, our picture and sculpture galleries, our theatres and scientific museums'. (There is more than a touch of Hampstead there.) We may think that rationalist attacks upon faith should not have an effect, that we ought in some way to deem them irrelevant. Since faith cannot be proved by reason, neither can it be disproved. That is indeed the case, but it would be insensitive in the extreme to persuade ourselves that the matter should end and does end there. For although reason cannot have the final say for faith, it nevertheless, as we saw, has its contribution to make, and we are bound to take account of reasoned attacks upon faith in God. Hans Küng gives good advice when he writes 'Belief in God is continually threatened, and – under pressure of doubts – must constantly be realised, upheld, lived, regained in a new decision.' Because faith is as it is, it must necessarily feel the force of attacks upon it. It is not like a juggernaut of a tank whose massively thick armour enables it to charge on confidently. Since it is part of the privilege of faith to be sensitive and aware of what others are thinking and saying on their journey through this life, it is not likely or possible that their arguments against faith will not make themselves felt. Not less grievous are those who have worked from within the camp of faith to erode its position, however good their intentions. All these assaults we must receive into ourselves and not evade. There are no 'answers' as such, and in this realm 'answers' can be much over-rated, often

turning out to be no answers at all. Only time will enable faith
to find itself undamaged at the heart, to reassert itself firmly
but gently, and carry on strengthened by surviving the latest
assault. God has a way of making himself known to us when
he discerns that we need it.

The life in faith then is not 'a calm sea and a prosperous
voyage', to borrow the title of Mendelssohn's overture, if these
words betoken a condition of invulnerable well-being. In that
event faith would be set apart from that struggle which is the
characteristic mark of the 'not yet' life, the life which is still
upon the way, ultimately indeed the mark of all life in this world.
It would in some way also be set apart from the hum-drum world
which, hum-drum or not, is very precious in the sight of God
and is the milieu which he has given to us for this life. It is
not intended so to be set apart. And if it is not all sunny seas
and plain sailing, are there not rewards here and now? It is
possible to think so exclusively about the assaults on faith and
the hazards which beset the life of faith, that the great and real
rewards of faith become overshadowed. That would be a fatal
mistake.

The greatest, the most incomparable, indescribable and
priceless reward of the life of faith is in the *knowledge of God's
love for us, the companionship of Jesus Christ and the inspiration of
the Holy Spirit*. It may be, and indeed is, the case that God has
set us at a distance of knowledge from himself. But, as we shall
see even more clearly when we come to think of faith and prayer,
there is a cumulative conviction that God has made something
of himself known to us. It is not in open ways, ways to which
we can point in demonstration. Nevertheless it becomes
increasingly difficult to deny the presence in ourselves of a
knowledge of God which is not a matter of human invention
and imagination but has been given to us. That is the first great
reward of faith. This is complemented by the second great
reward, which is *the experience of worship*. Worship is one vital
expression of faith and a crucial concomitant of it. It is thus
of the highest priority that it should be conducted in a
manner which inspires, exalts and strengthens rather than
distracts. Public worship is the most potent instrument of non-
verbal communication which lies in our hands. Dignity,
purposefulness, relaxedness, good movement, clear diction,

imaginative arrangements, use of varied voices, a deep prayer-fulness, a sense of drama – these are right and necessary ingredients in the best possible performance of public worship. Worship which is based upon these – and none of them is less than necessary – will refresh the souls of those who share in it with a renewed sense of God's wonder and love.

The third great reward of faith is the outcome of the first two, the knowledge of God and the worship of God. It consists in knowing ourselves as the objects of God's love and *therefore of having a grasp both upon our own identity and upon our place in the world's pattern.* Without wishing to be nihilists, many people today find it difficult to discover any meaning in themselves or in the world at large. Not surprisingly therefore they feel uncertain of themselves, uncertain of their own unique personality, unaffirmed in it; whilst at the same time the world itself has the appearance of being a series of random events, the most spectacular and photogenic of which get flashed upon the television screen. It is difficult to discover any pattern, or any way of interpreting these happenings as they occur. They are pictures lacking an overall frame. Faith cannot relieve us of the proper impact of the world's events, nor indeed of some of the ills which can afflict the human personality. But it can provide a base, a rock on which to stand in order to face the storms within and without. It can provide a touchstone to which we may bring things for assessment. It gives us a home for belonging and a community of faith in which to grow. And that is a gift of incalculable value.

What shall we say, in conclusion, about continuing in faith? It is, and must be, for ever a life of living from moment to moment –

> 'I do not ask to see the distant scene;
> one step enough for me'.

We must live in the present moment, find God in the present moment, be supported by his grace and power in the present moment. But there is also a cumulative quality in the life of faith, a sense of being built up, a grateful recognition of what *has* been given, and therefore hope of what *will* be given. Recognition and hope are at the core.

CHAPTER 6

Enemies of Faith

If the title of this chapter has an adversarial sound, that is not by accident. If there are enemies in any department of life, it is better that we call them so than by some squeamish euphemism. Enemies do not come only in physical or military form. They come in the form of ideas, most powerfully in the form of ideas. Sometimes ideas have auxiliaries called 'vested interests', but usually they are strong enough to fight on their own without assistance. To give to enemies their proper title helps those who need to stay awake and watch, to be on the alert and to guard themselves and others. Nor are we exaggerative in using such language. It is true, nothing truer, that God leaves us utterly free, free to respond to him in faith or not, to live the life that flows from faith or not. We are stamped with this freedom. But there are those in the world who reckon nothing of any freedom that may in theory be the birthright of their fellow-humans. Compared with the possession of power and with the successful domination of others by the imposition of ideologies, freedom is of little account, at best thrown amongst the litter of things marked 'unimportant luggage: not wanted on the voyage'. Thus to speak of *enemies* of faith is only sober sense.

If you are besieged in a castle, you can be attacked by frontal assault, by hordes of enemy charging across the plain and up to the castle walls with their arrows and engines and grappling-irons. Or you can be attacked from within by secret tunnellings which undermine the foundations of the castle and gnaw away at its structure. Or you can be attacked by oversight and accident, by careless servants who allow sacks of flour to grow mouldy with weevils or let some poisonous herbs get into the soup. The enemy who attacks by frontal assault is always preferable. He is out in the open, it is clear what he is trying to do, and you can have a measure of respect for him. You can even feel pity for some of his host, since you know that they are not really hostile to you at all but have been drummed up into his array to make up the numbers and so launch a more effective attack.

It is certainly possible to discover enemies of all such types amongst the enemies of faith. As with the defenders of the castle, the battle is always easiest against those who have come out of their camps and taken up a clear and open position against your own fortifications. But in that sector a certain stalemate appears to have been reached, with both sides agreeing that, in the nature of things, neither can make headway against the other, neither can look forward to a spectacular victory. Time was when the defenders of faith quaked behind their battlements, as Nietzsche hauled up a great engine (called Also Sprach Zarathustra) and Marx and Engels fired flaming manifestos which couldn't easily be put out, and then some of the philosophers found a new and penetrative missile called 'the verification principle' which looked as if it might reduce the defenders to a meaningless shambles with all their communications systems put out of action. But despite all such alarms (and a gentleman called Darwin who tried to reduce the defenders to a state of shame by addressing them as a load of monkeys), the defenders have found themselves still holding their position, a little flustered and flushed and also surprised, but indubitably there and Mattins and Evensong still being said and the bell rung.

At which point we had better take leave of the defenders on the walls of the castle – they have had a good innings and have had a few cracks at one or two of the enemy, but they have served their function and we must bid them farewell. It is time to turn our attention to those enemies of faith which are more dangerous because they are less obvious (like the tunnellers beneath the castle), and also more diffused. There are factors, influences and trends spread throughout today's society and its thinking, which are not easy to gather together in an identifiable form – and yet it is very necessary that we should try to do so. Much is a sort of deposit, a precipitate, which has filtered through into many of our assumptions. And we must remember how influential assumptions are, just because they are assumed, taken over, without critical assessment, breathed in with the air.

One of the great watersheds of our time was undoubtedly the work of Sigmund Freud, the true founding father of modern psychoanalysis. Freud was a man of great courage who found his final haven in this country after the Nazi takeover of Austria in 1938. It is a tribute to the pervasiveness of his influence that his name is often on our lips, even if only in the use of the cliché 'a Freudian slip'. In fact comparatively few people are acquainted with his work at first hand, which in itself is not surprising. Yet there is a widespread assumption that Freud proved that religion (a term not so far used in this book) was only a projection of our desires and had no objective foundation in truth. It is also assumed that Freud was an atheist as a result of his psychoanalytic studies. The overall conclusion is that you cannot at one and the same time take Freud's discoveries seriously and have faith in God.

What are the facts? Freud, a Jew by race and religious upbringing, was an atheist before he made the major discoveries about the functioning of the human psyche. In his writings he makes it clear that, whilst he has unearthed much in the way of infantile attitudes towards religion and many instances in which religious attitudes were acting as a substantial hindrance to healthy psychic development, the truth of religion, that is the trustworthiness of faith in God, can never be disproved by psychoanalytic discoveries themselves. It is of course of some significance that Carl Jung, the great Swiss analyst, who dissented from some of Freud's more extreme positions, retained faith in God, though along somewhat idiosyncratic lines.

Freud's discoveries therefore cannot properly be taken as in themselves hostile to faith. But it cannot be doubted that they have made their contribution to the assumption by many persons that there is an incompatibility between the findings of psychoanalysis and faith in God, a conclusion never claimed by Freud himself and indeed not sustainable. But does that mean that those who have faith write off the conclusions of Freud and others in so far as they purport to throw light on the workings of the human psyche? Anyone who has some acquaintance with this field knows that it is, in the best sense, experimental; that it proceeds by observation and the building up of case-histories, and that it is therefore difficult to speak of fixed and final positions. But that certain key and invaluable discoveries have been made, which may now be treated as established, should not in any way be denied. On the contrary they should be welcomed, grasped and used. The most obvious instance of what may now be regarded as established beyond doubt is the formative influence exercised by the experience of the earliest weeks and months and years of anyone's life. Whilst those who have faith in God may disregard the negative claims against such faith which are ignorantly based upon Freud, they may and should see the insights of the great analysts as illuminating and valuable friends, not to be regarded uncritically, but welcomed for what they contribute.

It is natural to turn from Freud, who was not through his own work a true enemy of faith, to a human problem upon which he cast much light, and which can indeed be an enemy of faith in practical terms. This is the experience of *depression*. This is one of the most widespread and most painful of human mental afflictions. It is still widely misunderstood and unappreciated for what it is, partly no doubt because in many instances it is possible for the sufferer to maintain an appearance of normality, even though all may be grey and ghastly within. It is not our purpose here to offer a full description of depression in its symptoms and causes, only to draw attention to the widespread occurence of depression and to see what effect it has upon our ability to maintain faith in God.

It is clear that when we speak of depression as an enemy of faith we are not seeing it as something which is deliberately launched against faith by any agent who wishes to destroy the ground of faith. We can talk of depression as an enemy of faith only because it has the ability to cause great distress and pain to people of faith who suffer from it.

From the point of view of those who suffer from it the prime characteristic of depression is that it is an *all-engulfing experience*. It takes a person over entirely and without remainder so that it is a total condition. In its least virulent form it simply places a grey film over the whole of the mental horizon, so that everything is covered with it and the whole sense of reality and normality appears a stage removed. When anyone is attacked by depression in a degree which merits the description 'clinical', it is often such as to paralyse action and make it impossible for a person to perform even the most routine and straightforward of tasks. In depression people are unable to react in anything like their normal way to stimulants, are incapable of enjoyment, and lose confidence. Those who suffer from depression will see this as a rough and ready description but not a false or misleading one.

What is the effect of depression upon a person's faith? Although depression may arise from one of a number of different causes, physical or psychical, or from a combination of them, it is the *result* with which we are concerned. *The effect of depression is virtually always to make a person feel that their faith has left them.* The more that anyone is still tending to identify faith with a sense of assurance, the more certain this is to be the case. For depression simply removes all feelings and leaves in their place only an overall negativity, a sense of hopelessness and of the general pointlessness of things – the Latin phrase 'taedium vitae', weariness of life, sums it all up well enough. Our sense of faith is *always* the first casualty. There is a certain irony in this: at the very moment when we most need the support which our faith is accustomed to give to us, it has left us, gone absent without leave, let us down. But, of course, it cannot be otherwise, because of the all-engulfing nature of depression. Our sense of faith does not have a privileged position, which mysteriously enables it to be outside the engulfing wave. If that were possible – a strange and unreal possibility when we really think about it – the depression would lose its sting; for then there would be some part of us which could sit apart, independent, and observe what is happening to us. But that it just what cannot happen. When we are depressed we are in the depression with the whole of ourself, hook, line, and sinker, lock, stock, barrel and everthing else. That is what is so devastating. That is why, *quite unavoidably*, we lose all sense of having any faith in God.

So, what do we do to combat this most insidious and frightening of enemies, which seems able to ambush us without warning? In this, as in many other circumstances, it is wise to talk to another person, someone with the requisite knowledge and experience to give counsel which carries weight. They may be in a professional capacity – in certain instances they will need to be – or they may not. The essence is that there are things which others can say to us which we cannot say to ourselves. We need to hear another voice speaking than our own, the words of another in our ear. And what should we be told? In the matter of faith, it needs to be pointed out to us gently but firmly that nothing has changed objectively since we were attacked by depression. The world has not changed its nature, nor has God changed his love for us. Nor has our own altered sense of things been confined to the matter of our faith. It has covered everything else – our relationships, our family, our loves, our work – everything. We must assume therefore that our loss of faith is part of the unified phenomenon, not something in its own right. So far as we can, we should do what we normally do as specific practice of our faith, e.g. prayer and worship – but not expect that they will mean anything to us in any normal way; and we must be very gentle with ourselves. We must just 'go through the motions'. It is not dishonest, as anyone advising can see. It is the only course of action possible. And when sooner or later, the depression lifts, then our faith will be there – has been there all the time only our sense of having it has been removed. If we have somehow managed to struggle on with the empty shell of our practice, we shall discover in due course that our faith has been strengthened by our having endured the desolating experience. Anybody who has this responsibility of advising someone in depression should place an unyieldingly insistent emphasis upon the unchanging reality of God's love.

Depression is one of the experiences which brings home to us personally that the world has a very dark side to its life. It is frequently referred to as 'the problem of suffering' or 'the problem of evil'. For those without faith, and not seeking it, these things are not, at least in terms of purely objective logic and reason, problems, although their human impact is universal. But for faith in God they are indeed problems, and in that sense suffering and evil are enemies of faith. Their existence, their palpable and clamorous existence, poses problems both subjective and objective, both practical and theoretical. The impact of suffering can disturb or remove faith, or prevent its ever being born. A young priest, two days after his ordination, called at a house where the son of the family, only in his twenties, had just died of a sudden malignant disease. What could he say, and of what could he speak (he was not yet old enough or wise enough to understand the virtue of silent and supportive presence)? Where is God at such moments, in any sense which has reality and impact? And what is present in the flesh and blood occurrences of life, what makes the needle of suffering so sharp, is what also makes the objective question so sharp for faith. The facts of evil and suffering are evident and omnipresent in the world. Do they not argue with sickening conclusiveness that this universe cannot be the creation of a loving God, and therefore of any God in whom we may properly and justifiably have faith? Do not evil and suffering make other enemies of faith seem pygmies?

We could well allow evil and suffering a fuller say – there is, alas, only too much material which could be adduced, from the Inquisition to the Holocaust, from the tip at Aberfan to the Herald of Free Enterprise in Zeebrugge harbour, from Hiroshima to the latest flood in Bangladesh. There are times when we scarcely know which way to turn for the multitude of tragedies and disasters and sheer evils. Public tragedies have their counterparts in private lives millions of times over. But the case has been made, and it will grow no weightier by multiplication of instances. It is a formidable case, filled with the fierce, raw, rending, bleeding stuff of human experience, urgent and immediate.

What answer can faith make? It is both possible and important to state that the freedom of the world to suffer is the cognate of the freedom which, we believe, is the gift of God to humanity. You cannot have the second without the first. An ordered world, one which contained no possibility of evil and suffering within itself, would not be the creation of God's love, and it would be no world for us. There is only one world worse than a world in which suffering and evil can and do occur; that is a world in which they cannot, if such a world can be conceived. Nevertheless, the argument posed by evil and suffering is against the possibility of God at all, since a credible God must be a loving God, and the suffering in the world is a sure contradiction of such a God's being the world's creator.

It is not the part of a book such as this to attempt to engage in a prolonged theological defence of the truth of God's love in the face of the undeniable facts of evil and suffering. That has been done most ably eleswhere.[1] Here we may remark that it is exactly at this crucial point that *Christian* faith in God diverges fundamentally from all other faiths. Crucial is the exact word, since it is the *Cross* of Jesus (Latin, crux-crucis) which holds any key to the problem of suffering which may exist in this world. When in Chapter 2 we were thinking about the *initiative* of God in the person of Jesus, we spoke of Jesus carrying this initiative in himself. We saw that in due course he suffered death by being impaled upon a wooden cross and that from that death he passed into the life of God himself. But the full faith of Christians is that God was in Jesus, that, in St. Paul's words, 'God was in Christ reconciling the world to himself'. Nothing else has ever constituted the faith of those who believe and trust in Jesus as the Christ of God, from those first communities which produced the Gospels onwards. In some mysterious but utterly real way, the death of Jesus is the work of God; it all happened within the purpose and will and foreknowledge of God. But that death is also God's sharing in the suffering of the world. It is God's exposure of himself to hazard and weakness and the worst that the world can do. It is the suffering of the God who does not simply behold this world with compassion but makes himself a part of it to the utmost limit of its suffering experience. Because the death of Jesus is also the suffering of *God,* it has a universal quality. Whatever it effects, it effects for all that goes before it in time and for all that will come after it. It effects it for the large-scale, massive sufferings and tragedies, and for the individual ones, away in their quiet corners of sadness. Where will you go for the signs of the huge sufferings – to Auschwitz or Treblinka or the endless cemeteries of the Somme or Verdun? Where will you go for the signs of the untellable roll of the individual tragedies and sufferings of the world, to any quiet churchyard, pausing perhaps by the headstone of a child, pausing to let the imagination supply all that inscription cannot? But truly, you would need to enter an innumerable host of hearts ever to learn one tiny fragment of the tale of the world's suffering. But none of it, not one tiniest portion of it, lies finally outside the effect of the suffering of God in Jesus upon the Cross outside the walls of Jerusalem on a Friday afternoon (as we should say) so many centuries ago. The death and passing to life of Jesus are, for those who trust them, the promise of God that all that is ill will be made good, all manner of things become well.

In terms such as these faith makes answer to the fact of the world's pain as seeming to deny the goodness of God and therefore God himself. It does it in the only way which truth will permit, by showing that it was for no other purpose than to deal with what constitutes precisely 'the problem of evil' that God came into the life of his own creation in the person of Jesus. It could not be other. For the evil, expressed in death, is that which makes *the* great insoluble for the world, *the* question mark over its whole life as holding meaning. Beside it all enemies of faith pale, and if Jesus has indeed overcome death – and therefore evil and suffering – there are in the end no other enemies, only phantoms.

[1]See especially John Hick, *Evil and the God of Love,* 1966.

CHAPTER 7

Faith and Prayer

Prayer is, quite simply, what we do as a result of having faith
in God. That is to say, if we have to choose *one* practice which
flows from faith and expresses faith, that practice is prayer. For
prayer is not one practice among many, still less is it a pursuit
for the specially pious. It has been remarked that 'prayer is not
one of the things which we ought to do'. It is not in that sense
a thing to do at all. Nevertheless it is a practice, it is *the*
practice of faith in God. Again that does not imply that there
will be no other practices: a monstrous idea, an encouragement
to pietism, a good step towards a well and truly cloistered faith.
Where would be works of mission and of charity, love and
service of one's neighbour? But it is still true that prayer is *the*
practice of faith, that stems from faith, and that it provides the
context for all others.

But what is prayer and how do we embark upon it and
pursue it? In a sense we have already given a definition in the
opening words of this chapter – prayer is what we do as a result
of faith in God. If it is objected – quite reasonably – that that
is so wide a definition that it could embrace almost anything,
we would reply that it is better at this stage to have our
conception too wide than too restricted. To say that prayer
is what we do as a result of our faith in God makes the
fundamental point that prayer is the direct outcome of our faith.
We pray because we have faith, and without faith in God prayer
has no meaning and no justification.

Faith in God carries with it the implication that between God
and ourselves there is a relationship. If we are God's creation
and are loved by him, it cannot be otherwise. The relationship
cannot avoid existing. It is there; and if it is there, it is there
to be explored. If God is God, then all the hopes of each one
of us must be found in coming to know him and in coming
to share in his life. Before everything else with which our life
has to do – growth, education, work, marriage, family, success,

pursuits – it has to do with God. God is the source and heart of our life, therefore the meaning and fulfilment of our life must of utter and absolute necessity be found in *attending to God.* If we do not attend to God, if we do not as it were turn ourselves towards him, there is no likelihood that we shall come to know him. So, again, prayer is attending to God and turning to God.

But – because we are attempting to be honest in all that we say – let it at once be made clear that expressions such as 'attending to God' and 'turning to God' must have an unique connotation. God is not like any other person and, as we saw earlier, he is not *a person,* though he is *personal* and *more* (i.e. not less) *than personal.* We are entering into relationship with *Being* itself, with the one God. There is nothing else that we engage in which can be compared with this, and well-intentioned but necessarily inadequate comparisons are probably more misleading than helpful. If anything is sui generis, of its own unique kind, it is not of true help to say that it is like something else. It isn't. But the phrases 'attending to God' and 'turning to God' do nevertheless denote something real – indeed something very real indeed, the most real of all. And once we understand this, however mistily, we shall understand something else as a result: *the enterprise of prayer cannot fail.* How, we ask, can that be?

In the relationship of prayer there are two parties, God and ourselves. In the relationship, as in all else, God never removes our freedom and never overwhelms us with his presence. Despite the indescribable disparity between us, God does not oppress us with the awfulness of the inequality, or show up our poverty with his riches, or our weakness with his power. At the same time nothing can alter the plain truth that the two parties in the relationship are not on the same footing as each other, for one is creator and one is created, and those terms stand for a gulf of existence which we can never approach describing. So, when we turn to him and attend to him, God waits for us and waits upon us. But through his Holy Spirit he is already in us and he is already empowering us, though with such restraint that we have no sense of being taken over. We are at each and every moment free, but at the same time it is true that the whole relationship is *in God.* We are starting to

real-ise our sharing in the life of the Holy Trinity into which
we were brought sacramentally at our baptism. The grace and
the power are all God's but in our prayer we are free agents,
truly free, for there are no fictions with God. Yet because the
grace and the power are his, and because, however hiddenly,
they are all available to us, it is the plain truth that *the
enterprise of prayer cannot fail.* It may seem to our limited
perceptions, perceptions which are moreover deeply affected
by other aspects of our human frailty, that the enterprise *can*
fail; but the truth is that it cannot. A major part of the
difficulties which arise in prayer come from the apparent
disparity between this truth and the actual experiences which
come to us as we try to pray.

When we start to give ourselves to prayer in a deliberate and
extended way, moving from 'saying prayers' to something more
reflective, meditative, contemplative and silent, God cheers us
and encourages us with a sense of his presence. (This is the
counterpart to our first experience of coming to faith). We may
believe that, being familiar with what manner of beings we are,
he knows that we shall need every encouragement if we are not
to faint and fail at the outset. This will continue probably for
some while – there is no hard and fast rule, only a very general
pattern of experience. But at some point the sense of God's
presence with us when we pray will become diminished. We
start to find the going harder, and there are fewer rewards of
deepened feelings, exaltation and delight. Quite simply it
becomes harder to pray, harder to spend the amount of time
which we had resolved to spend in prayer. We may consult
someone more experienced than ourselves, which is a practice
of common-sense. But, although they are reassuring to us, the
actual prayer becomes no easier. In fact the opposite: it seems
to become more and more bare, more and more shorn of any
positive feelings of consolation and reward, of being warmed
by God's presence. (The process which we are describing may
well cover a period of some years.) What is happening to us?
It *feels* as if nothing at all is happening, as if we were engaged
in a non-event or an exercise of nothingness.

What is happening is, contrary to all appearance, extremely
positive. Against all likelihood it represents very substantial
progress in our prayer and therefore in our relationship with

God. But in order to see that this is so, we need to reflect further upon what causes the apparent contradiction: our experience seems all negative and we are assured that it is really positive. The fact is that when we encounter this experience in prayer, when everything seems bare and shorn and, yes, bleak, we are actually starting to live in the true pattern of faith. Prayer is *the* activity of faith; prayer is faith expressing itself in its most direct form. Therefore, sooner or later, it is in prayer that we are going to experience the whole condition of living in faith in its most undiluted and unprotected form. And, as we saw when we thought about continuing in faith, much of the actual experience of living in faith is in feeling that we have no faith. There we learned that we should not identify faith with a felt sense of assurance. Here we are learning that lesson again in the setting of prayer. We are learning that a great deal of our prayer takes place in the equivalent of the desert, very different from the comparatively lush pastures in which we fed at the outset. But we also learn, gradually and painfully, that the desert is a place with its own validity, its own safety and even its own strange reassurance. (You could say that all this represents a sort of spiritual realpolitik).

Some of the most illuminating words about the true meaning of this sort of experience in prayer were written by a member of an enclosed contemplative religious community, whose members spend much of their lives in prayer: 'It is because contemplative prayer has nothing to do with the itch for experience, and everything to do with a patient and persevering will to receive truth and to be made love, that it is hard, dark, combative and boring. It confers not a sense of well-being or release, but a broken heart. Its sincerity is tested not in finding life a bit more bearable but in the willingness to keep coming back for more – for a deeper self-knowledge and a further bearing of reality. The contradictions, false starts and set-backs by which a life of prayer develops correspond quite simply to the basic paradoxes of the Christian faith – joy through suffering, life through death, victory through failure, peace through conflict – and the stifling negatives by which we know our remoteness from God have to be acknowledged and endured in dependence on him if they are to be healed and transfigured by the drawing of his love.'[1] Patently and beyond all doubt those words come from a life and heart devoted to God in prayer. They are paradoxical in themselves, for they use many terms which are negative and yet confer freedom and reassurance. How refreshing and liberating to have someone from such a background calling prayer boring! The heart of the passage lies in its saying plainly that it is by contradictions, false starts and set-backs that a life of prayer develops. All negatives and yet yielding a positive result! The absolute opposite to all our normal ideas of success! We can continue with our prayer which often seems so negative in confidence that it really is such as God can use.

There are several important further implications of Sister Isabel Mary's words. First, the primary purpose of prayer is not for experience, but to enable God to continue his work of giving us truth and making us love. That does *not* mean that we are never to have experience of God in prayer, but that that is as God wills. It is not the *primary* purpose of prayer, and it is not within our power to achieve it, since it is a gift of God himself. What we *can* achieve is to give our time and our wills and our hearts to prayer, confident that if those are given to God, he will *always* use them. We return to the foundation truth that *the enterprise of prayer cannot fail*. Second, her words drive us back to recalling what we said earlier about the role of God himself in our prayer. He is there, he is in us, he is actually using whatever is offered to him. He may use it obscurely, silently and mysteriously, because we can never detect his work at the time, and we can never observe him in operation. But we come to know, humbly and firmly, that he has used our prayer. So thirdly, we know the effectiveness of our prayer by what we can observe *outside* the actual times of prayer. If, looking back over a period of time, we can detect that, despite the many obstacles which our sins and weaknesses have interposed, we have grown in love and come to a deeper understanding, we may believe with some good reason that God has been enabled to continue his work in us. And, however negative our experience may seem to be within prayer itself, we come to know that there is a difference between life with prayer and life without prayer. One aspect of that is well illustrated by William Temple's observation 'When we pray, coincidences happen; when we don't pray, they don't.' And there is a fourth implication of the words of Sister Isabel Mary: we are the worst judges of the quality of our own prayer. It is when, in subjective terms, that our prayer seems most cloudy, most empty, most fruitless and most unrewarding, that it is beyond doubt being most productive in the hands of God. For the plain and undeniable fact is that we are choosing to spend ourselves and that time for God in that way, rather than in any one of a dozen different ways in which we might otherwise spend them. Our prayer is our choosing and what follows from it. More is happening in it and through it than can ever touch our consciousness. It is indeed the prayer of faith.

What is the practical result of this? We should feel profoundly encouraged to go on praying – obeying the words of the Lord who taught his friends that 'they ought always to pray and not to faint'. It is not as if we are unready to accept interior hardship in prayer, so long as we know that it is to good purpose, that it is all within the knowledge and purpose of God and that he is using what we offer. The truth is that, in the end, only one thing is necessary for prayer: that we should go on praying and be content to leave it all in the hands of God.

[1]Sister Isabel Mary SLG, 'The Reconcilers: II', *Crucible*, May 1970.

CHAPTER 8

Having Another Person

In the course of these pages we have several times referred to seeking advice or consulting an experienced person. Although these references have formed only an incidental feature of our discussion, they have been made, but without any indication of how they might in practice be pursued. It seems right therefore to try to say something about how to find help in our pilgrimage of faith. A great deal can, of course, be gained from books – even from this one – and the habit of reading books about God and faith and prayer is invaluable. But sometimes it is helpful at least to have experienced guidance in the choice of books, a judgement of what will accord well with our needs at the time. And further, there are things to be gained from live discussion which cannot be had from books alone. In this matter, books are never a substitute for person-to-person consultation.

What is the guiding principle in this matter? Its roots are to be found in what was said earlier concerning continuing in faith and the community of faith. There is the foundation truth which underlies the Church as the Body of Christ and the community of faith but which goes far beyond their confines; *we all belong to each, we all interdepend, we are infinitely closer to one another than our conscious perception can tell us.* The mutual coinherence of human beings with each other is one of those archetypal truths about ourselves which are gradually borne in upon us as we grow in experience of life. This universal truth about the whole human race is brought to explicit expression within the community of faith and there given a new force and significance. Linked with this all-important truth about us all there is another: *we all need to express ourselves.* That phrase can be misleading and can bring back memories of school-reports which contained some such comment as 'He or she is at present rather lacking in self-expression'. We must firmly put away all such associations and take hold of a much richer meaning of self-expression. It is to do with ourselves as our complete selves, the whole of our conscious and unconscious being. That being requires to be *expressed,* that is to

say for its fulfilment it needs to be able to go out from itself, to
be projected, to go forth – to where? It can only be to another
person. Here we are speaking of a universal human requirement
which gets fulfilled in a great many different ways and forms. But
we must also note that for many people this requirement of their
nature is frustrated through lack of opportunity, through the
virtual isolation in which many are forced to live, even though they
are surrounded by other people. (Bernard Levin gave a classic
description of this condition when describing the closing scene
of the great French film 'Les Enfants du Paradis' in which
Baptiste vainly pursues Garance, his adored lover older than
himself, through the crowds en fête: 'Desolation amongst gaiety,
separation in the midst of unity, the heartbroken in counterpoint
with the carefree.')

If our need for self-expression is part of the guiding principle
underlying our consultation of another person, another part is
that *in the life of faith we are not intended to be alone.* That is both a
theological truth and a matter of commonsense. To think
otherwise is unbelievably wasteful – wasteful of truth and wasteful
of opportunity. The richness and joyfulness of faith are only fully
realised in the community of faith, and within that community
it is our calling to support one another. When we are attempting
to follow the way of faith in God, it is natural that we should look
for someone who will advise us and observe our progress. There
are many hazards upon the road of faith, many opportunities for
becoming discouraged or mistaken. There are aspects of ourselves
which it is difficult for us to see and understand. There are things
which God is bringing to pass in us which it needs another
person to discern and point out. There are hints about possible
fresh ways of praying, a fresh balance to be found between various
parts of our Christian practice, new endeavours which it might
be right for us to undertake. In any other walk of life it would be
axiomatic that we should place ourselves in the way of learning
from one who was more experienced than ourselves and also
particularly equipped to guide us. It can come down to the basic
truth that there are things which can be said effectively to us only
by another voice than our own. There is an effective ministry
simply in virtue of being another person to whom we can express
anything that we want. But a wise and evaluative experience of
the ways of God and of the demands and pitfalls of living in faith

is worth rubies; and there is a particular insight which comes from a life of prayer. It is one of the astonishing features of life within the Church – and it applies to all the Churches in varying degrees and within their respective idioms – that we do not resort to others for spiritual support and guidance more than we do. Our failure to do so is an all-round loss to the life of the community of faith.

One reason for our failure to get spiritual guidance for ourselves may lie in the fact that it is not offered to us deliberately enough. Much of this work must lie with members of the clergy, though not with them alone – the Church has had and does have distinguished lay spiritual guides and writers, of whom Evelyn Underhill, Baron von Hügel and Olive Wyon were notable examples; and the members of religious communities frequently offer a valuable resource. But many English Christians conspire to ensure that their clergy fulfil every function except that which they were ordained to fulfil, namely the care of souls. And the members of the clergy often connive at it. It need not be so. Let the members of the clergy make plain that they regard this as amongst their highest priorities, and there will be response. Let the members of communities of faith make plain that they wish for this spiritual care and nurturing and guiding, and they will stir the members of the clergy to provide it. Whilst it is to be expected that any member of the clergy should be ready to do this, it is also a fact that certain priests and ministers feel a particular calling to exercise a ministry of this kind and to devote much time to it.

Nevertheless, it is not just as simple as that. Discrimination and sense are needed. Not everyone is suitable, by temperament or by gifts or by calling, to receive spiritual help and guidance on an individual basis. There are fine people of faith, whose attitude to faith and to life in general is very simple and who could not cope with talking to someone else about themselves and their life of faith and their prayer, except possibly within the setting of sacramental confession. But many people, who would shrink from personal, individual guidance, would benefit from it very greatly in a small group, where they would find a setting of support in which guidance could happen easily and naturally and be shared with others. The sort of groups which we considered in the context of continuing faith can very well serve this purpose, and a good many members of the clergy today find that this setting works well for a lot of people; and that in time such people are trusting enough to be ready to reveal a good deal about themselves and their needs.

At the same time it is of great importance that individual spiritual guidance should be available generally and that those who are specially equipped to provide it should be widely known. It is important for the spiritual integrity of the whole community of faith, the Church. Without it there is a great gap, a fearful failure in realism, an absence of that attitude which might be characterised as 'holy businesslikeness'. If people are not expressing a need for individual spiritual guidance, at some point at least in their journey, what does that say about the earnestness of their desire to grow in their faith in God? Here the community of faith needs to learn from the practice of other bodies such as industrial concerns, or the armed forces. If there is a job to be done, you must receive the training necessary. Faith and prayer are in a true sense a job to be done, and we need the training for them.

It is possible that some persons are inhibited from seeking individual guidance not only by possible embarrassment at talking about their inner selves and their life with God, but also by fears of surrendering their freedom into the hands of another. It must be said that there have been times when these fears were justifiable – one thinks of how St. Teresa of Avila suffered from unwise and overbearing confessors. There are certain traditions in the Church today which like to exercise rule and sway over the lives of individuals. But it can be firmly said that the whole tenor of spiritual guidance is away from any wish to dictate to a person what he or she should or should not do and towards listening carefully in order to discern both the particular temperament and spiritual character of the person and also what God appears to be saying *to* that person and doing *in* them.

A wise spiritual guide can bring us great profit and great encouragement, sometimes acting as a restraint and – much more rarely – as a goad. Most often his or her role (women, it needs hardly to be said, provide excellent spiritual mentors) is to act as a sounding-board so that a person may have reflected back to them what they are heard to be saying. Very often in the Christian tradition spiritual guides have been entitled 'spiritual directors'. So long as they are not thought to direct, the title may stand, and it certainly betokens a firm and businesslike approach to the whole matter, in keeping with our times and with the vital nature of what is in hand. Very often their role is to reassure us – to tell us that all is well, despite what we may feel to the contrary. When our praying feels like a directionless jumble, they can tell us that it is perfectly all right. From the outside we can see that these things are so, though from the subject's viewpoint it cannot be perceived: the complementarity of the objective and subjective views is of first-order importance. So we can be given advice such as that given in a letter by the late Father O'Brien of the Cowley Fathers to a nun in an enclosed community who for years had suffered the utmost darkness and desolation in her prayer: 'It is a very painful trial – but I want to say to you definitely: you have faith – you do pray – you do possess God and he does possess you.'[1] We all need someone at some time to tell us that all our negatives are really all right.

Does the spiritual guide or director act also as a counsellor? Part of wise discernment is to perceive the true nature of any person's needs, and in what area they fall. Complementary to this is to know where your own particular skills and training begin *and end*. It is one thing for example to have some knowledge of the rudiments of pyschology, it is quite another to try to act as an amateur and self-appointed psycho-therapist. Spiritual guidance and counselling certainly overlap; you cannot deal with someone's faith and prayer in isolation from the rest of their lives, and it would be artificial and unhealthy to do so. But there are clear distinctions between the two skills, and they should not be confused. It is likely that anyone who has had a training in counselling will be at times a better spiritual guide, but the two roles should not be unwittingly and indiscriminately mingled. It is important that a swift discernment should be made of those who are suffering from observable neurosis or psychosis, so that appropriate advice may be given. This does not entail that the spiritual guide should immediately withdraw from the relationship, only that the advice given should be appropriate. It ought to be said that the classic spiritual guides and writers have always been also psychologically perceptive.

Are there texts for spiritual guides? Perhaps Jesus with the woman of Samaria at the Well of Sychar in Chapter 4 of St. John's Gospel provides a pattern, whilst much of the work of a spiritual guide is summed up in the words of Emerson: 'We mark with light in the memory the few interviews we have had in the dreary years of routine and sin, with souls that made our souls wiser, that spoke what we thought: that told us what we knew: that gave us leave to be what we inly were.'

[1]A Cowley Father's Letters, 1962, p. 87.

Postscript

No book, least of all this one, can in itself and by itself cause faith to grow where there is no faith. But for those who are seeking, a book, even this one, may provide some contribution, some words in season, some pointers and encouragements, even a little provocation. Any book about faith in God will only be another part of the ongoing stream, something that rose briefly in its time and will soon go its way into oblivion, having in God's grace performed a tiny function. Let the writer, by way of envoi offer three quotations which have long accompanied him. First from Miguel de Unamuno: 'Those who say that they believe in God and yet neither love nor fear Him, do not in fact believe in Him but in those who have taught them that God exists. Those who believe that they believe in God, but without any passion in their heart, without anguish of mind, without uncertainty, without doubt, without an element of despair even in their consolation, believe only in the God idea, not in God Himself.'[1]

And then from that great religious genius, Rudolf Bultmann: 'Faith is exercised in the abandonment of one's certainty; a man therefore can never achieve it as a work of his own purposeful action, but he experiences it only as something effected by God. In the hour of decision it is shown whether faith was one's own work or the gift of God.'[2]

Finally from the English New Testament scholar Edwyn Clement Hoskyns: 'To believe is to apprehend human action, all human action, in its relation to God; not to believe is not to recognise the only context in which human behaviour can be anything more than trivial. The man who believes recognises that all human behaviour is by itself and in itself incomplete. The man who believes knows that God fills up his incompleteness, and that, in filling it up, he makes the human act a thing which is wrought in God.'[3]

[1]Miguel de Unamunol, *The Tragic Sense of Life*, p. 193.
[2]R. Bultmann, *The Gospel of John*, p. 447.
[3]E.C. Hoskyns, *The Fourth Gospel*.